Our America

Sam Hancock

Series Editor
Mark Pearcy

Contents

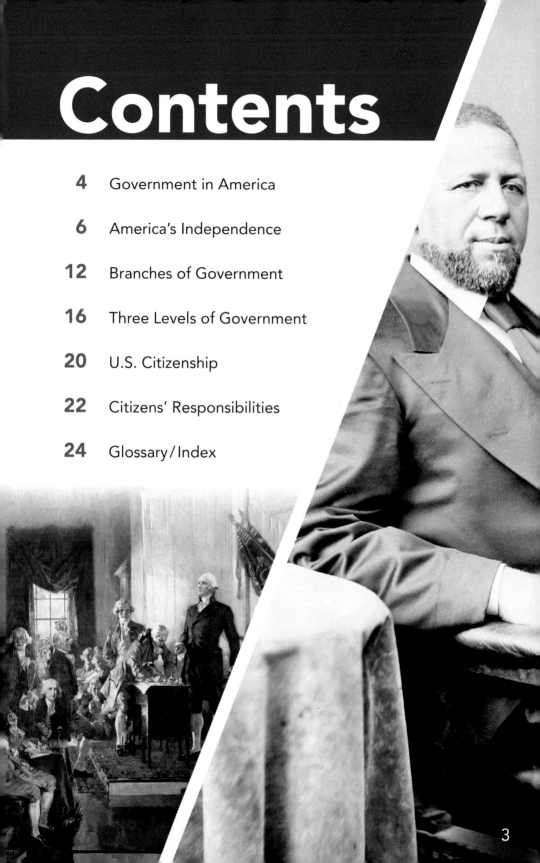

3

Government in America

Have you ever wondered how a government works, who works in a government, or what a government does?

The role of a government is to serve its citizens and protect their rights. A government is a group of people who manage how a country, state, or city is run. Citizens are the people who live in a country, state, or city who have their rights protected by its government.

The United States was founded as a democracy. A democracy is a political system in which representatives are elected by citizens to run the government.

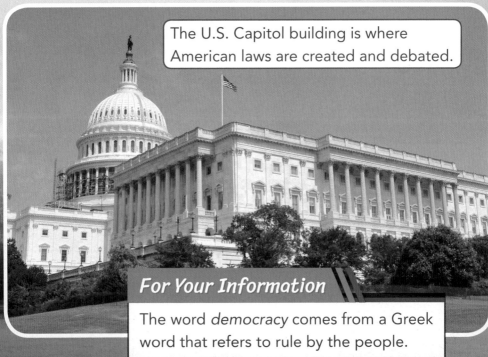

The U.S. Capitol building is where American laws are created and debated.

For Your Information

The word *democracy* comes from a Greek word that refers to rule by the people.

The Iroquois Confederacy

Before European contact, there was already a system of government in the land that became the United States. This was the Haudenosaunee Confederacy, which was also known as the Iroquois Confederacy. It included the Mohawk, Oneida, Onondaga, Cayuga, and Seneca cultural groups. The Tuscarora cultural group joined in the 1720s.

The Hiawatha Belt is an important symbol to the Iroquois Confederacy. The squares and tree stand for the original five groups.

Like a democracy, the purpose of the Iroquois Confederacy was to give an equal voice to all of the groups involved. Each group chose one elder to represent its members. The elder had one vote on all matters put to the confederacy. Each decision the confederacy made had to be unanimous, which means that everyone had to agree to it. The Iroquois Confederacy is still active today. It continues to work to protect the rights of American Indian peoples.

America's Independence

Before the United States became an independent nation, it was made up of 13 British colonies. A colony is an area under the control of another country, which is often far away from the colony it rules. The people who live in a colony are called colonists. The 13 British colonies were New Hampshire, Massachusetts, New York, Pennsylvania, Rhode Island, Connecticut, New Jersey, Delaware, Maryland, Virginia, North Carolina, South Carolina, and Georgia.

Each colony had its own government, but these governments were controlled by King George III of Great Britain. George III had not been elected. He had become king upon the death of the previous **monarch.**

Great Britain introduced new taxes to the colonies in 1765. The colonists did not like paying high taxes to a government in which they had no representation. They decided to take action.

King George III was the monarch of Great Britain until his death in 1820.

Declaration of Independence

In 1776, a group of colonists wrote the Declaration of Independence to tell Great Britain that the colonies wanted control of their governments. In the declaration, they wrote that "all men are created equal" and that everyone's basic rights were "unalienable." This meant that an individual's basic human rights and freedoms could not be denied or taken away. Those basic rights are life, **liberty,** and the pursuit of happiness.

For Your Information

At the time that the Declaration of Independence was written, the word *men* was used to refer to both men and women.

This 1818 painting shows five of the founders presenting the first draft of the Declaration of Independence to the Second Continental Congress.

The U.S. Constitution

After the United States won its independence from Great Britain, the founders wrote the Articles of Confederation. The articles gave only limited powers to the **federal** government. The federal government was responsible only for matters of war and **commerce** between states. The articles were written in 1777, but they were not **ratified** until 1781.

By this time, it was clear that a stronger federal government was needed. To address this problem, the Constitutional **Convention** was held in Philadelphia, Pennsylvania, in May 1787. States sent delegates, or representatives, to help write a constitution for the country. A constitution is a document that states the rules for how a political organization will be run.

The Constitution was ratified by all states in 1789 after the Bill of Rights had been added. The U.S. Constitution outlines the ways that the American government works and the basic laws of the nation. It was written to support the rights and freedoms of U.S. citizens.

Bill of Rights

Amendments help make the Constitution clearer. The first ten amendments, known as the Bill of Rights, protect personal freedoms and rights, put limits on government power, and specify what powers belong to the federal and state governments.

The Declaration of Independence, the Constitution, and the Bill of Rights are considered the Charters of Freedom. The Charters of Freedom are the cornerstone of the American government and guarantee the rights of every citizen.

For Your Information

Since 1787, more than 9,000 amendments have been drafted, but only 27 have been approved. In order for an amendment to be added to the Constitution, three fourths of all the states must ratify it. This process can take a long time. For example, the Twenty-seventh Amendment was considered for more than 200 years before being passed in 1992.

George Washington was elected the leader of the Constitutional Convention.

9

Reconstruction Amendments

The passage of the Thirteenth, Fourteenth, and Fifteenth Amendments, or the Reconstruction Amendments, is an example of how the Constitution has been adapted to protect the rights of American citizens. Reconstruction was the name of the period of time after the Civil War.

The major cause of the Civil War was the use of slave labor in the Southern states. Abolitionists were American citizens who wanted to end slavery. They worked hard to convince the public and President Abraham Lincoln that the Constitution should be changed to provide equality for African Americans.

After the war, the Reconstruction Amendments were passed. The Thirteenth Amendment abolished slavery. The Fourteenth Amendment guaranteed citizenship for all American-born people. The Fifteenth Amendment granted voting rights to all African American men. However, these laws were not **enforced,** and African Americans did not obtain their guaranteed rights until the 1960s.

This 1867 illustration shows African American men registering to vote.

Nineteenth Amendment

For more than a century after the Constitution was approved, women in the United States did not have the right to vote. The women's rights movement pushed for equality, including women's suffrage. Suffrage is the right to vote in elections. A constitutional amendment calling for women's right to vote was introduced in 1878, but it did not pass.

Susan B. Anthony (right) and Elizabeth Cady Stanton helped found the National American Woman Suffrage Association.

In 1890, the National American Woman Suffrage Association was formed. The group **lobbied** politicians and protested in front of the White House. All of these actions gained attention for women's suffrage.

During World War I, from 1914 to 1918, American women joined the workforce in large numbers for the first time. They were filling the jobs of men who were fighting in the war. Women played a significant role in the workforce during the war.

Public opinion started to change about women's roles in society. President Woodrow Wilson put his support behind amending the Constitution. The Nineteenth Amendment was ratified in 1920, granting women the right to vote.

Branches of Government

The U.S. government is divided into the legislative, executive, and judicial branches. The legislative branch writes bills that can become laws. Bills that are approved are signed into law and carried out by the executive branch. The judicial branch reviews and evaluates the laws.

The Constitution has a built-in system of checks and balances. This system ensures that the government does not become too strong or threaten citizens' rights. Each branch can limit, or check, the actions of other branches. No single branch has too much power. In sharing power, the branches must work together. They must also work within the limits of the Constitution.

Checks and Balances

Legislative Branch	Executive Branch	Judicial Branch
Known as Congress and made up of • House of Representatives • Senate	Made up of • President • Vice president • Cabinet	Made up of • Supreme Court • Other federal courts
Congress passes bills and controls the budget.	Can **veto** laws	Reviews laws
The Senate approves presidential appointments.	Appoints judges	Can declare laws and presidential actions **unconstitutional**

Legislative Branch

The legislative branch is called Congress. It represents Americans' interests and creates laws that will affect everyone in the country. Congress has two houses: the House of Representatives and the Senate.

The House of Representatives is made up of people elected to represent a district in their state. They serve for two years. States with higher populations have more representatives. This is called proportional representation. Wyoming, the least populated state, has a single representative, while California, the most populated state, has 53 representatives.

The Senate is made up of elected officials called senators. Senators serve for six years. Each state has two senators, regardless of its population. This is called equal representation.

For Your Information

Senator Hiram Revels was the first African American elected to Congress. He represented Mississippi from 1869 to 1871. He spoke out against racial **discrimination** in schools and in the railroad industry.

Executive Branch

The executive branch is made up of the president, the vice president, and the cabinet.

As head of the executive branch, the president has one of the most powerful jobs in the world. The president directs national defense, foreign policy, and the government. The president can recommend new laws and veto ones passed by Congress. The president works closely with the vice president and the cabinet to put federal laws in place.

The vice president is the head of the Senate and is a member of the cabinet. Cabinet members advise the president and lead the various government departments. These departments include the Department of Transportation and the Department of Agriculture.

Franklin D. Roosevelt

When Franklin D. Roosevelt (FDR) was running for president in 1932, he promised to help the United States get out of the Great Depression with a "new deal." Partly due to the success of his New Deal programs, FDR won a record-setting four terms as president. After that, the Twenty-second Amendment was passed. It limits a president's time in office to two terms.

Judicial Branch

The main part of the judicial branch is the Supreme Court. The Supreme Court is made up of nine justices, including a chief justice. Justices are appointed for life by the president and approved by the Senate.

More than 8,000 cases are submitted to the Supreme Court every year. However, only about 60 to 80 are heard. The decisions of the Supreme Court are final.

Judicial Review

Just before the presidential election of 1801, the government appointed William Marbury as a justice of the peace. However, that government lost power in the election. The new government did not give Marbury the job he had been promised. Marbury then took Secretary of State James Madison to court. The Supreme Court decided that Marbury should get the position. It also ruled that Madison and the government had gone against the Constitution by denying Marbury his job.

The *Marbury* v. *Madison* case was the first time the Supreme Court had decided whether an action by the other two branches was constitutional. The power to decide this is called judicial review.

This is the first photograph ever taken of Supreme Court justices all together. It was taken in 1869.

Three Levels of Government

In the United States, there are three levels of government: federal, state, and local.

Delegates at the Constitutional Convention of 1787 agreed on a cooperative system. This system divides power between the federal government and the state governments. This political system is called federalism. The federal government makes laws that affect all Americans, while state governments make laws that apply within their state boundaries.

The Tenth Amendment states that powers not granted to the federal government are reserved for states and citizens. Like the federal government, each of the 50 states has its own constitution. Each state also has three branches of government.

Local governments, such as towns and cities, are granted their powers by the state. They are responsible for local services, such as emergency services. They are also responsible for taking care of public works, such as transit and roads.

The House of Representatives meets in the House Chamber of the U.S. Capitol building.

How Laws Are Made

Congress makes federal laws that are to be followed by everyone in the United States. A law begins as a bill. The process begins when someone comes up with an idea for a new law.

How a Bill Becomes a Law

A member of Congress introduces a bill for discussion.

↓

Representatives (if the bill is introduced in the House of Representatives) or senators (if the bill is introduced in the Senate) vote to decide if the bill will go to a committee.

↓

The committee discusses possible changes to the bill.

↓

The house in which the bill was introduced decides whether to support the bill with the committee's changes.

↓

The bill goes to the other house of Congress to be discussed and voted on.

↓

If both houses vote to accept the bill, it goes to the president, who can sign or veto the bill.

| The president signs the bill. | The president vetoes the bill. |

The bill becomes law.

The bill is sent back to Congress, where it is discussed further.

State and local governments can make their own laws. Once a state or city makes a law, the law applies to all people living in or visiting that place.

Let's look at an example of a federal law, a state law, and a local law to see how laws are made.

Federal Law: Americans with Disabilities Act

The Americans with Disabilities Act bans discrimination against people who have disabilities. The act requires public buildings and transit to be **accessible.** Companies must make workplaces accessible to employees with disabilities as well.

The Civil Rights Act of 1964 was passed to protect the rights of all Americans regardless of race, age, religion, gender, or political opinions. However, people with disabilities were not included in this act. In 1986, the National Council on Disability recommended a new act specifically protecting the rights of people with disabilities.

The bill was introduced to the Senate in 1988 by Senator Tom Harkin of Iowa, whose brother was deaf. The bill was passed by both the Senate and the House of Representatives and signed into law in 1990.

The Americans with Disabilities Act was approved by President George H. W. Bush.

State Law: Ralph M. Brown Act

Open government is the idea that the public should know about and have a say in what the government is doing. In 1950s California, there was concern that local government groups were trying to avoid public attention. People believed that city councils, county boards, and other groups were holding secret meetings.

California State Assembly member Ralph M. Brown introduced a bill to protect the public's right to attend and participate in local government meetings. The bill was passed by the State of California in 1953. The law now bears Brown's name.

Local Law: San Francisco's Tobacco Laws

Local governments are concerned with issues that affect people within their boundaries. These issues include health and safety concerns.

San Francisco's city council has laws in place to protect the health of its citizens and visitors from the effects of tobacco smoke. The laws ban smoking in public spaces, at outdoor events, and at the entryways of buildings.

U.S. Citizenship

People born in the United States are citizens. People who move to the United States can also become citizens through a legal process called naturalization. Having citizenship allows people living in a country to have the full rights and responsibilities promised by that country. The Constitution guarantees that the federal government will protect every citizen's rights and treat all citizens equally.

Citizens of the United States have the right to a fair trial, to vote, and to stand for public office, among other rights. Citizens' responsibilities include supporting and defending the Constitution, defending the country if needed, and obeying all laws.

Being a citizen of the United States means more than following laws. It also gives people the right to participate in their community and the democratic process, including voting in elections once they reach the age of 18.

Before becoming U.S. citizens, people take part in a ceremony. They take an oath to support and defend the Constitution.

Citizens' Basic Freedoms

The First Amendment of the Constitution sets out the basic freedoms of U.S. citizens. These are essential principles of democracy in the United States.

- Freedom of Religion: Congress cannot name an official religion of the country. Congress also cannot prevent individuals from practicing their religion.

- Freedom of Speech: Individuals have the right to express their opinions and ideas without fear of government restriction.

- Freedom of the Press: Media, including newspapers, television, and Web sites, have the right to communicate ideas and opinions.

- Freedom of Assembly: Individuals have the right to gather with others to share ideas and concerns.

- Freedom to Petition the Government: Individuals have the right to address the government without fear of getting into trouble for sharing their opinions or complaints.

Citizens' Responsibilities

Besides outlining citizens' freedoms, the Constitution also states U.S. citizens' responsibility to defend the Constitution and live by its laws. This includes respecting other people's beliefs and opinions.

Citizens have a responsibility to participate in government. If elected officials do not do a good job, citizens have the right to share their opinions with the people they elected.

Get Involved!

There are many ways you can participate in your government even if you are not old enough to vote. You can consider

- joining your school's student council.

- sharing your views with a button or a bumper sticker.

- reading and learning about issues that are important to you.

- collecting signatures on a petition to raise awareness of an issue and to bring about a change.

Participating in government helps a democracy work. When citizens think their elected officials are not representing their interests, they often get more involved.

If there is an issue in your community or school that you want fixed, there are ways you can let your local officials know. Look online to find out who your local officials are. Most government officials have a public Web site with contact information.

You can then write a letter or an e-mail outlining your concerns. Always consider offering a solution to the problem that you think would work. There may be many issues your local officials are considering, so it never hurts to offer some help!

Glossary

accessible: able to be used

amendment: an addition or change to a legal document

commerce: the exchange of goods through buying or selling

convention: a large meeting of people to discuss particular interests or concerns

discrimination: the unfair and unequal treatment of a certain person or group of people

enforce: to carry out and make sure laws are being observed and obeyed

federal: relating to a central or national government

liberty: the power of choice; freedom

lobby: to try to influence people in power

monarch: an unelected head of a country, such as a king or a queen

ratify: to officially approve through voting or signing

unconstitutional: not done according to the Constitution

veto: to reject

Index